You Write

Non-Fiction Writing for GCSE English and Other Examinations

Gordon Michael Sutton

© Gordon Michael Sutton 2020

All rights reserved. No part of this publication may be reproduced, stored in a retrieval system, or transmitted in any form or by any means, electronic, mechanical, photocopying, recording or otherwise, without the prior permission in writing of the publisher, except in the case of brief quotations embodied in a book review.

ISBN: 978-1-9160147-2-5 (Paperback)
ISBN: 978-1-9160147-3-2 (Kindle)

Typesetting – Chris Moore

Contents

How to use this book.................................v

Introduction 1

Section 1 – Genre to Genre 5

The Non Fiction Writing Genres................10

Number 1 – an Article..........................11

Number 2 – an Essay...........................12

Number 3 – a Leaflet..........................19

Number 4 – a Letter...........................21

Number 5 – a Speech..........................25

Section 2 – Headlines, Straplines & Sub-Headings 29

Section 3 – Audience & Purpose 37

Section 4 – Tone 49

1. Angry......................................51

2. Enthusiastic................................52

3. Frank/Honest...............................53

4. Impassioned 54

5. Optimistic 55

Section 5 – Discourse Markers 63

Section 6 – Planning 71

Non Fiction Writing Exemplars 83

Write an Article 84

Write an Essay 89

Write a Leaflet 93

Write a Letter 98

Write a Speech 102

How to use this book

I've written and designed this book to be as authentic as possible, filling it with plenty of my own examples of tackling the writing process itself as well as completed responses to typical exam questions. There are also detailed commentaries on each of the five exemplars of **non-fiction/transactional writing** to help you understand some of their key strengths and to identify the sort of features they contain.

My goal has been to develop your confidence, enthusiasm and motivation as writers, so I've worked hard to make sure the content of the book is as creative and attractive as possible, including the careful selection of interesting and appropriate photographs.

The book has been divided into *six* sections:

- Section 1 – **Genre to Genre**

- Section 2 – **Headlines, Straplines and Sub-Headings**

- Section 3 – **Audience and Purpose**

- Section 4 – **Tone**

- Section 5 – **Discourse Markers**

- Section 6 – **Planning**

Each section follows a similar step-by-step approach, with careful explanations of all of these key aspects for producing effective non-fiction/transactional writing and the sort of strategies that can be used to achieve this.

Most important of all, the book offers you regular opportunities to have a go at non-fiction writing – hence the title – *'You Write It'*.

These 6 sections are then followed by **Exemplar Responses** to Exam Questions plus a **Commentary Box** on each of the exemplars; *Article, Essay, Leaflet, Letter* and *Speech*. The key below helps to simplify the design and structure of the book.

Key

- Summary of key points and ideas

- Instructions

- Exam questions or titles

- Examples of my writing + exemplar responses to exam questions

- Commentary on Exemplar responses to exam questions

- Space for your written responses and ideas

Why not follow me on:
Instagram : **@secretsofenglish**
Twitter : **@english_secrets**
YouTube : **SecretsOfEnglish**

In addition, you can contact me directly at the following:
info@secretsofenglish.co.uk

Introduction

The title of this book refers to **non-fiction writing** which is also known as **transactional writing**.

Remember though, this is not narrative or descriptive writing which I've dealt with in my first book – *'You Write It – Creative Writing for GCSE English and Other Examinations'*. This means that you will need to think and write in completely different ways when producing the various types of non-fiction writing that will be asked of you in your English examination.

Take a look below at what your GCSE English Language examination will need you to be able to do when it comes to **non-fiction/ transactional writing**.

You will need to be prepared to write one or more of the following:

- An article
- An essay
- A leaflet
- A letter
- A speech

No matter which of the above *genre* you're writing in, you need to be able to do so for a particular *purpose*. These could include:

- To argue
- To explain
- To instruct/advise
- To persuade

Finally, you need to be able to write your piece for a particular *audience* and examples of this might include the following:

- A group of students your own age
- The readership of your local newspaper

So what is non-fiction or transactional writing?

Non-fiction or transactional writing deals with what's real; with facts, figures, ideas, arguments, opinions, and more. The crucial thing to remember about non-fiction or transactional writing is that we're not in the business of making stuff up anymore. We're dealing with the real world rather than the world of the imagination as is the case with narrative or descriptive writing.

And because we're dealing with the sort of things that matter in the real world, the look and feel of non-fiction writing is entirely different. Above all, any non-fiction writing we produce should remind us of the first three letters of the alphabet – A, B, and C – it should be *Authentic, Businesslike*, and *Credible*.

A is for Authentic.

Your writing should sound genuine and heartfelt. It should reflect your own views and ideas. Keep an eye on expressing yourself as honestly and directly as possible and you won't go far wrong.

B is for Businesslike.

Your writing should be crisp and clean with none of the flourishes you might have needed in your creative writing. Although you will need to use some quite specific language features – for example, rhetorical questions, the rule of three, or a direct address to your reader. I'll deal with these later in the book.

C is for Credible.

Whether you're arguing your case, offering your views, or trying to convince or persuade, you need to present yourself as credible. As someone who has ideas that are valid, genuine and worth reading. You will need to be able to organise these ideas clearly and effectively to help boost your credibility.

Section 1

Genre to Genre

Genre to Genre

You're going to need to be pretty versatile in your GCSE English exam and be able to move with confidence from one writing *genre* to another in the non-fiction writing section.

You need to be able to apply yourself to writing a **letter** just as easily as you would when writing a **speech, article, essay** or **leaflet** for instance.

Sometimes you may have to choose between writing in one of two possible genres. Or you may, in fact, need to be able to write in any one of five possible genres. Check with your English teacher about what your particular exam syllabus specifies and requires of you.

Getting Your Head Around *Genres*

First, you need to be clear about which **genre** the examiner wants you to write in. Read the question carefully – it should tell you quite explicitly which genre it is that you need to produce.

Second, you need to be just as clear about what writing features or conventions are unique to each particular genre.

Don't let the term *genre* or *genres* alarm you; it's quite straightforward really!

Perhaps the story below might help in the first place.

Watching *Westerns* with my *Grampa*

My grandparents had a black-and-white television when I was young and my Grampa liked nothing better than to sit and watch his favourite films on it. These were what we now call '***Westerns***', and I'd happily sit and watch them with him. No matter what the specific film was, I soon came to recognise the sort of things that I'd expect in the film – the conventions, or features associated with the ***genre*** of the '***Western***'. These included some of the following:

- Struggles and hostility between the cowboys and the local, native American Indians – this often involved the native American Indians circling the settlers' wagons and lots of arrows being fired
- Gun fights – sometimes in a ramshackle town, sometimes on horseback, sometimes up in the hills
- Maybe a bank robbery in the small western town
- The local sheriff coming to the rescue
- Plenty of scenes showing the cowboys at work and riding their horses
- Scenes showing activity in and around the teepees of the native American Indians

The thing is, once you'd seen one Western, you'd pretty much seen them all – they seemed to follow a tried and tested pattern, or formula. For the viewers, my Grampa and I included, much of the enjoyment came from the fact that we could recognise these typical features or conventions with each film we watched.

Now Think About Your Own Viewing

Choose *one* of the following *genre* on our screens and list the features or conventions you'd expect to see:

- Detective/Cop Show – eg, **Bosch, Broadchurch**, or **Columbo**
- Science Fiction Series – eg, **Dr. Who, Humans**, or **Star Trek**
- Cartoon/Mystery – eg, **Scooby Doo, Batman** or **Danger Mouse**

....

....

....

....

....

....

How was that? Did you manage to figure out what makes your tv show fit into a particular genre? Hopefully, the sort of features you identified will not just appear in one episode of your show, but will also be present across all of its episodes. As viewers, we take pleasure and enjoyment from these familiar and recognisable features.

You can use the same approach and be able to recognise the features and *conventions* expected in the various non-fiction writing **genres**, too, and put them to work in your own writing!

YouTube: SecretsOfEnglish

The Non Fiction Writing Genres

Article — Essay — Leaflet — Letter — Speech

First – let's start by pinning each *genre* down and explaining what exactly it is and what features it should contain.

The common denominator in the picture above is obviously that each item is a piece of fruit. But as you can see, each piece of fruit looks very different. They also feel different and certainly taste different too.

All the writing we're going to look at has the common denominator of being a piece of *non-fiction/transactional* writing, but as you will discover, each genre is quite different to the next.

Number 1 – an Article

An **article** can be written for a few different media formats such as newspapers, blogposts and magazines. It's not that important which one you're asked to write for as you will need to follow similar guidelines and approaches whichever one it happens to be.

What's really important is that it's a piece in which your views and opinions are expressed on a topic without necessarily trying to persuade your reader or readers. The purpose of an article is really to *explain* your views on a particular topic.

You're going to need to start by including a ***bold, eye-catching headline*** which signposts what the article is going to be about.

This is usually followed by something called a ***strapline*** which should provide a condensed version of what your article is going to be about. Don't gloss over this – think carefully about how you can use it to provide a neat, shortened version of the article as a whole. It should be a helpful springboard into the article for your reader, or readers.

If the headline and the strapline are key steps 1 and 2, the critical 3rd step when writing an article is your ***opening paragraph***. It's here that you can let your reader, or readers, know where you stand on the topic as well as making a confident step forward into the article by explicitly acknowledging the wording in the question's title.

After this, it's all about getting down to the business of expressing your ideas and thoughts, paragraph by paragraph, for the remainder of the article.

The main body of your article, as written in the paragraphs mentioned above, also needs to include some ***sub-headings*** to indicate the various sections and ideas as your article moves forward; they act a bit like signposts along the route. Finally, they should also help to summarise ideas at different stages of the article.

- Your views, ideas and opinions expressed without trying to persuade the reader
- A bold eye-catching headline
- A strapline underneath the headline which condenses what the article is going to be about
- An opening paragraph in which you let your reader know where you stand on the issue
- A well structured series of paragraphs in which you develop and expand upon your ideas
- Some sub-headings written at appropriate points in the article

See Exemplar No.1 –

"Social media has a completely negative effect on people's lives and should be banned."

Write an article for a broadsheet newspaper in which you explain your point of view with regard to this statement.

Number 2 – an Essay

'The best thing we could do is introduce compulsory national service for all 16 year olds in the UK.'

Write an essay, explaining why you agree or disagree with this statement.

Just take a moment to read the question above.

It's exactly the sort of question you could be asked to complete when tackling an essay as a piece of non-fiction writing. As you can see, it starts with a statement that is likely to provoke one of two distinct viewpoints in students being asked to write the essay – in short, you'll either *agree* or *disagree* with the statement.

In fact, there are two other possible responses a student might have.

First, they might actually ***strongly*** agree or ***strongly*** disagree with the statement.

Second, they mightn't actually care less one way or the other.

Whatever the response, your job when writing an essay of this sort, regardless of the question/statement, is to simply state your views.

Notice that at no point does this question ask you to persuade your readers around to your point of view.

In some ways, the process of preparing to write an essay is almost as important as what you're actually going to write.

Look at the steps in the process below:

- Whether you agree, disagree, or have no obvious views on the statement in the question, it's a good idea to try to brainstorm your thoughts on the subject – perhaps putting these down into a simple mind map
- Having done this, you ought to have a reasonably good idea where you stand on the statement in the question
- Next, weigh your ideas up carefully and decide what would be the most logical, straightforward sequence for presenting them in your essay. This should allow you to create a simple outline for your essay – a sort of route map from introduction to conclusion
- How about taking your argument for a test drive? Have a go at the 'elevator pitch' approach. Imagine you've only got the time between floors to tell the other person in the lift what you think about the statement; this will have the benefit of helping you to summarise your ideas nice and concisely and to weigh them up before committing them to paper
- As part of this process, it's really important that you give some careful consideration to any opposing views to your own on the topic, and jot these down to at the planning stage
- It's worth paying special attention to creating a powerful introduction – one that's going to rouse your readers

Here's that question from the start of this section on Essay writing again:

'The best thing we could do is introduce compulsory national service for all 16 year olds in the UK.'

Write an essay, explaining why you agree or disagree with this statement.

Now would be a good time to grab a piece of A4 paper to have a go at brainstorming and mind-mapping your ideas on this question. Don't forget to include some opposing views, too.

If you've followed this and are able to use the thinking behind the process in the exam, you should be ready to start writing.

Just as with writing a speech, the trick with writing an essay is to follow a 3 part structure – **introduction, mid-section**, and **conclusion**.

Although each section is as important as the next, it's still a great idea to devise a strong introduction that engages your reader from the get-go.

What makes a good introduction?

Here are a few of the techniques you could use to write a bold, effective introduction set out below.

- Start with a question – perhaps a rhetorical question – one that's going to challenge your readers
- Start with a bold statement – one that sets out your stall clearly and unambiguously – leaving the reader in no doubt where you stand on the subject
- Maybe you could start with a pertinent set of facts or figures that have the effect of being thought-provoking, as well as helping to build your credibility as the writer on this topic
- Perhaps even start with a simple, but memorable anecdote that hooks the reader's attention straight away – as human beings we're naturally curious, so when a writer shares something in an anecdote, we're likely to sit up and pay attention

Whichever way you choose to write your introduction, you mustn't forget to make a clear reference to the statement that's in the actual question.

Here's the question from the start of this section on Essay writing again:

'The best thing we could do is introduce compulsory national service for all 16 year olds in the UK.'

Write an essay, explaining why you agree or disagree with this statement.

Using some of the ideas you brainstormed earlier and having had a chance to reflect on the question carefully, now it's your turn to try to write a bold, introductory paragraph. Don't forget to refer to the bullet points in the yellow box above.

....

....

....

....

....

....

....

....

....

....

You now need to follow the **introduction** with a carefully structured and well written **mid-section** in your essay. Remember, the job of the mid-section is to expand in more detail on your main viewpoint. In addition, this is where you can demonstrate that you can recognise and acknowledge an alternative viewpoint.

What makes a good mid-section?

- The most important thing to remember here is to ensure that your ideas are all really well organised
- Draw on your earlier planning and brainstorming to identify the material that you have at your disposal

- As part of this approach to effective organisation you should work hard to create a sequence of ideas that makes sense to the reader
- As you might expect, well written paragraphs with one key idea per paragraph is what's required here
- In addition, remember that being able to write a really good topic sentence at the start of each paragraph will make all the difference
- To assist with the last point you should try to find ways of expressing yourself that manage to signpost and connect your ideas

You've already written your own introduction above so why not have a go at writing the next paragraph in your essay on the question we've been thinking about. Above all, this paragraph needs to have a good topic sentence that shows the direction of your thinking. Plus, it should also follow on logically from the introduction you've written.

....

....

....

....

....

....

....

....

....

Finally, a strong conclusion is required to bring your essay to a close.

What makes a strong conclusion?

- It's been important to use effective topic sentences in each of your paragraphs throughout the mid-section; it's now vital to start with a really good topic sentence here that begins the process of summarising your ideas

- You might want to consider using one of the following phrases at the start of your conclusion: 'In conclusion …', 'Overall…', 'Thus …', 'Finally …', 'As expressed …'

- Do not simply repeat what you've said already … try to pull your thoughts together by summarising them

- As part of the above, keep in mind that it's all about tidying things up in a neat package for your reader at this point

- Ensure you refer to some of the key words in the original question

- Remember – you should not try to bring up any fresh ideas in your conclusion

- A good conclusion should really be able to show your readers that you've done what you set out to do in your opening paragraph

- Your closing sentence should be your last word on the subject and hopefully leave your readers with something to think about

One thing you will have noticed in this section on writing an essay – there's no need for any headings, sub-headings, or addresses. It's all about the 3- part structure, written in clear sentences and paragraphs, expressing your view on the topic while recognising, acknowledging and dismissing alternative views.

See Exemplar No.2 –

Teenagers need to become more active if they are to lead healthier lives.

Write an essay, explaining why you agree or disagree with the statement.

YouTube: SecretsOfEnglish

Number 3 – a Leaflet

A leaflet is generally used to inform and/or persuade. If you're asked to write one in the exam, naturally you won't be able, or expected, to produce design-quality graphics and layout. It's the text of the leaflet that's important.

You will, however, be expected to show in your layout, some sense of the features that a leaflet would usually contain.

As you might expect, you will need to use a ***bold headline*** or ***title*** and a series or ***sub-headings*** throughout the leaflet. Remember, the sub-headings are there to help divide up your ideas and content to help your reader or readers make sense of them nice and clearly.

When writing a leaflet, it's entirely reasonable to use some ***bullet points*** where these might be appropriate. Naturally, it's definitely not a good idea to litter your leaflet with them though! Choose carefully when, and how, to use them.

In terms of layout, you may want to consider using some ***simple boxes*** around part of the text in your leaflet. There's no requirement to do so though.

Obviously, you can research what leaflets look like online, but another good idea might be to pop down to the nearest shop, train station or coffee shop where you'll often see lots of different leaflets lying around. It's worth browsing through some of them, perhaps even taking some home with you.

Which ones catch your eye? Make two piles of the ones that interest you and the ones that don't. Then try to work out why some appeal to you more than others.

You certainly want to avoid writing a leaflet that's dull or boring to read.

In addition, your leaflet should be as clearly written as possible and contain just the right amount of information.

In terms of some of the features you might want to consider using when writing a leaflet are the following:

- A limited use of bullet points
- In addition to the heading and sub-headings, it might be appropriate to number some of your sections in the leaflet
- Occasional use of BLOCK capitals – perhaps for sub-headings, or to add extra emphasis as appropriate
- You might want to devise some contact details at the end of the leaflet to help make it more real and authentic
- As with many other pieces of non-fiction writing, you should include plenty of factual material as well as some statistics to help add credibility to your leaflet
- The style of your writing should be fairly plain to help convey information in as straightforward and effective a way as possible
- Often in a leaflet, you might want to use a direct address to the reader using words such as 'you' and 'your', or perhaps even phrases such as 'your home' and 'your family'; repetition of these words can have quite a strong effect on the reader in terms of credibility and trust in the writer
- In addition to the last point, the use of words like 'us' and 'our' can often work to create a sense of a bond between the reader and the writer

See Exemplar No.3 –

Write a leaflet for visitors that explains how to get the best out of their visit to a local attraction.

Number 4 – a Letter

Writing a letter can seem strange or alien to many people these days. After all, most of us tend to rely on communicating by email instead. We just don't seem to write too many letters – whether to friends and family, or for business and formal purposes. And because the vast majority of our communication with other people is by email now, we've grown accustomed to the style and features that are appropriate to this particular form of written communication.

One big difference, of course, between writing an email and writing a letter, is that an email system provides you with an email address bar for the name of the person you're writing to. And when you receive an email from somebody you can see clearly the email address of the person who's sent it.

So, when it comes to letter writing, it will now seem strange to most of us to be required to write a couple of addresses out in full at the top of the letter – before we even get round to what it is we want to say in the letter!

Perhaps you're wondering how to set out these addresses.

And what about the fact that this is a public examination; you won't want to be revealing your home address for all the world to see, will you?

First things first.

With regard to setting out the addresses, **your** address should go at the top right of the letter. Then you should leave a one or two line gap and write the date underneath the address on the right.

Next, you should write the address of **the person you're writing to** on the left, about a line or two below where the line containing the date.

Here's an example:

33, Picasso Avenue,
New Eastwick,
Lanchester,
LA9 9AL

14th June, 2020

Ms.Garfield,
1, Brockson Road,
Darsley,
Lanchester,
LA7 7AL

Dear Ms.Garfield,

    I'm writing with regard to…

Hopefully the example above should clear the whole address thing up for you. I should point out that not only have I created a fictitious address for myself, but also for the person I'm writing to. This will be perfectly acceptable to the examiner when s/he sees your letter set out like this.

You should also note the way I've started my letter quite formally, using the words *'Dear Ms. Garfield …'*

Finally, I've indented a little when writing the first actual line of my letter.

Now it's your turn to have a go.

> **Imagine you've been asked to write a letter to the manager of your local supermarket; set out the opening of that letter below:**

So that's most of the layout of the letter covered; it's really a case of trying to familiarise yourself with it as best you can.

Now you can get on with the business of writing your letter in clearly written and well-structured paragraphs; typically around 5 or 6 of them. Think carefully, too, about the sort of language that's appropriate. It will often be a formal letter that you've been asked to write and your vocabulary choices should reflect this.

When bringing your letter to a close, you should write *'Yours Sincerely'* if you know the name of the person you've been writing to. If not, then finish with the words *'Yours Faithfully'*. Underneath this, you should put your signature and underneath this, print your name out clearly.

One final word of warning; please take care to use capital letters properly when setting out the address section of your letter.

> **See Exemplar No.4 –**
>
> Write a letter to the managing director of a local company requesting sponsorship to help purchase 100 new bicycles for use by the public across your town or city.

Number 5 – a Speech

First things first – you are **not** being asked to *give* a speech. You are simply being asked to write the words for a speech. The aim, or **purpose** of the speech might be to persuade an audience, or even to explain to an audience what your viewpoint is on a specified topic.

So you should think carefully about **the sort of language** you will need to use to achieve whichever goal you've been set.

You then need to look carefully at who the **audience** for the speech is going to be.

In the case of a speech given to people your own age – your *peers* – it's probably best to use *informal language*. On the other hand, if it's a more serious speech – let's say to a group of business people, or some sort of professionals – then more *formal language* should be used.

Another way to ensure you write a great speech is to think in terms of a **3 - Part Structure.**

Section 1 – a strong, personal start in which you introduce yourself to the audience and secure a connection with them and get them to warm to you!

Section 2 – a more detailed mid-section in which you open up and expand on your topic or theme. This section will need to be written in a particularly clear and logical sequence as your audience need to follow your argument and/or your ideas and be persuaded that what you're saying is true and makes sense.

Section 3 – a strong, coherent conclusion with a clear and succinct message. This should aim to be inspiring and include a ***call to action*** to your audience.

Here's a summary then of the sort of features you might want to consider using when writing a speech:

- Personal introduction to the audience
- Acknowledge the audience
- Authentic voice throughout
- Use of anecdotes to catch and hold the audience's attention
- Direct address to the audience – *"you", "your"*
- 3-part structure – beginning, mid-section, and conclusion
- Clear introduction of the theme or issue to be spoken about
- Expand on the theme and provides examples from own experience
- Informal language as appropriate
- Use of a central metaphor if possible
- Rhetorical question/s
- Connect with the audience to help to inspire them
- Appeal to the audience to share your vision or ideas
- Alliteration
- Facts and figures as appropriate to establish credibility
- Powerful, concluding appeal and *call to action*

See Exemplar No. 5 – *'Parks Are A Thing Of The Past'*

Write the text for a speech in which you outline your views on this statement

YouTube: SecretsOfEnglish

Instagram : @secretsofenglish

Twitter : @english_secrets

Section 2
Headlines, Straplines & Sub-Headings

Headlines, Straplines & Sub-Headings

If you find you're required to write an *Article* in your exam, then you're going to need to be able to create a bold *headline* and an effective *strapline* to sit underneath it.

And when it comes to writing a *Leaflet*, you'll also need to be able to use a *headline* here too.

As for *sub-headings*, these are required in an *Article* as well as a *Leaflet*.

It's definitely worth spending a little time giving some thought about how to create effective *headlines*, *straplines* and *sub-headings*. Getting these right in your exam could make all the difference and show the examiner you've really got to grips with the business of non-fiction writing.

So where to start?

Imagine for a moment you turn to the non-fiction writing question and you see something like this:

> *"Sitting downstairs on the bus is a total waste of time and is only for losers."*
>
> **Write an *Article* for a broadsheet newspaper in which you explain your point of view on this subject.**

Clearly this is not a serious topic; I thought it might be interesting to take a fairly frivolous statement like this and see how to set about creating a headline, strapline and some sub-headings.

The first thing to do might be to work out where you stand on the issue – do you agree or disagree with the quotation in the question?

Next, you're going to need to gather the evidence to support your point of view. Take a look at the box below which contains some notes in the form of bullet points; it's pretty clear which side of the argument I'm on I think you'll agree.

> Notes
> - Crowded downstairs – filled with the elderly & mothers with small children … not to mention pushchairs, buggies – plus it's noisy
> - Even more crowded – people can stand downstairs too
> - Gets stuffy and hot downstairs more easily
> - Views are restricted
> - Danger of ending up sitting over the wheels – uncomfortable/noisy
> - People who sit downstairs lack the imagination to climb the stairs
> - *Londonist* website specifically singles out seats upstairs as the best seats on the bus – with top position awarded to front seat on the right on the top deck!
> - Sitting upstairs – can check people out as they come upstairs or on pavement below – without being spotted yourself
> - Better views all round generally – scenic inner city
> - Sitting upstairs is where the *cool* people are

Equipped with such a varied set of ideas, I now need to figure out if I can pull my argument together into one common thread by identifying my main point.

For example, I may decide that it's all about the view from the top deck.

Or perhaps it's about escaping the crush downstairs.

It could even be about the idea that the top deck is for *cool* people.

I'm going to opt for the first argument – that **sitting upstairs is all about the view** which you just don't get on the lower deck of the bus. Now I need to be a little creative and think about how this argument, and the article as a whole, might be summed up in a bold, eye-catching headline so as to draw my readers in.

I'm going to need to think about the following possibilities:

- Using wordplay or puns
- Maybe think about using numbers in my headline
- Using alliteration
- Using emotive language to make an impact on the reader
- Being concise
- Having a clear, recognisable connection to the topic and to the article I'm about to write

So below is a first attempt at a headline that meets *some* of the criteria above:

Looking Good On The Top Deck

The first two words – **'Looking Good'** – use a little wordplay – to refer to the main point of my article, while the rest of the headline – **'On The Top Deck'** – is very clear, explicit, and self-explanatory.

Keep things fairly simple – and remember, you don't need to write the world's cleverest headline!

Now I need a **strapline** to sit underneath the headline. The purpose of the strapline is to explain and expand on the headline. Take a look at what I've written below and see what you think.

Looking Good On The Top Deck
It's not just the view that's better upstairs on the bus!

I've reinforced my main point about the fact that riding on the top deck of the bus gives you better views and I've also prepared the reader for the other points that I'm about to make in favour of the top deck over the bottom deck.

Now I should be able to get on with the business of writing my article.

And as I do so, I need to think about possible **sub-headings** that I can use throughout the piece. At this stage, I'm not actually writing the article here, so I'm just going to review the ideas in the yellow box above and devise a few possible sub-headings based on these.

They might include the following:

> Climb the stairs – escape the crowd!

> Breathe more easily

> Where the cool people sit

> A smoother ride

> Best seats on the bus!

As you can see from my five possible sub-headings above, they can help provide the reader with a concise summary of what's coming next.

They almost act like signposts, helping the reader see which direction the article is going in. Now it's time to try this approach for yourself based on the exam question below:

> *"Suitcases on wheels should be banned."*
>
> **Write an Article for a broadsheet newspaper in which you explain your point of view on this subject.**

Step 1 – Decide whether you agree or not. Then jot down the ideas to support your **viewpoint** in bullet-point form.

Step 2 – Decide which is your main point and write a **headline** based on this.

Step 3 – Write a **strapline** to go underneath the headline.

Step 4 – Review your bullet points and devise a series of **sub-headings** that you can use in your article.

Step 1: Agree/Don't Agree – ideas to support my viewpoint

-
-
-
-
-
-
-
-
-
-

Step 2: From the ideas above, decide on my main point & write a headline

Step 3: Write a strapline to go underneath the headline

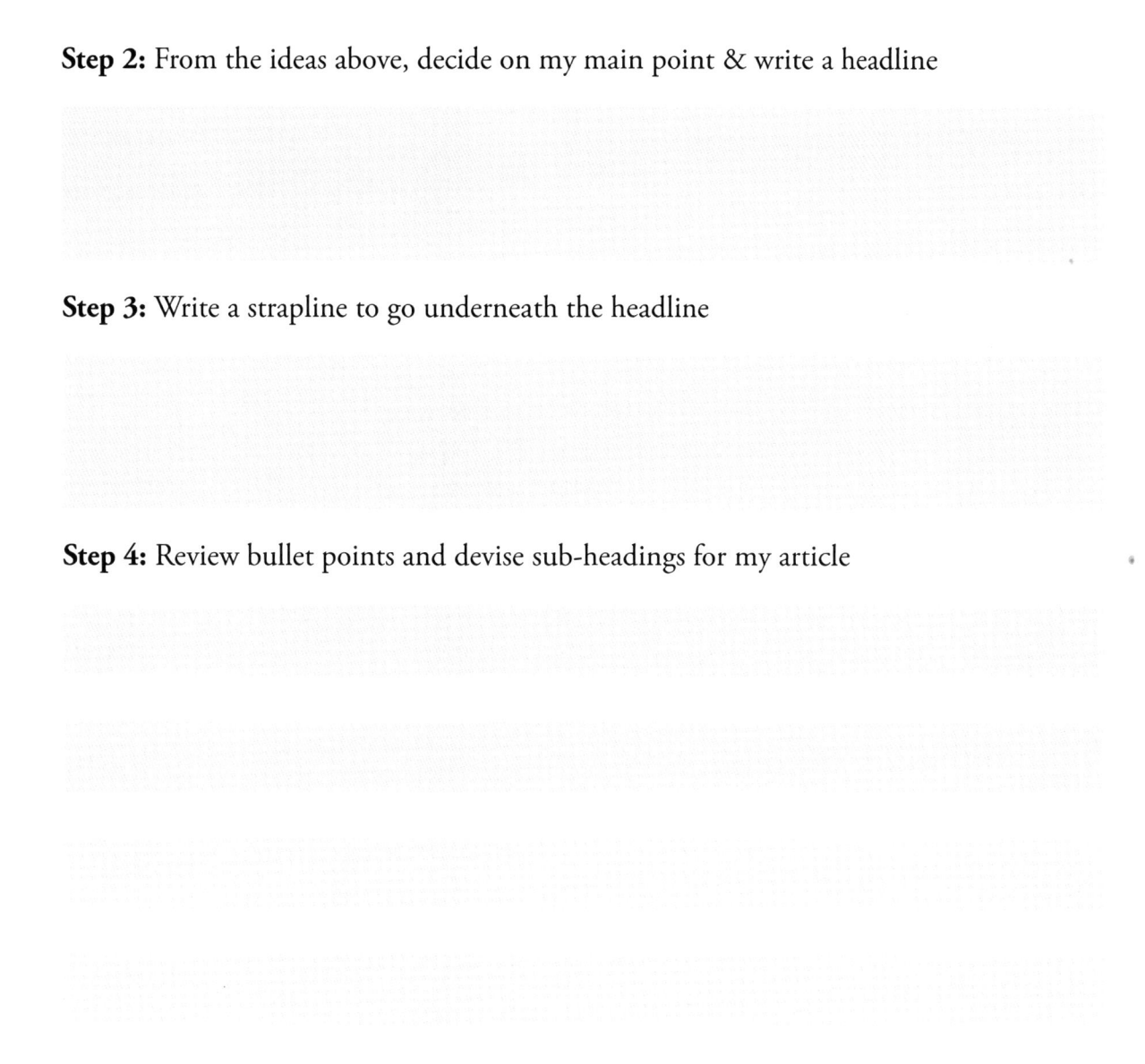

Step 4: Review bullet points and devise sub-headings for my article

Section 3

Audience & Purpose

Audience & Purpose

When you're asked to produce some ***non-fiction/transactional writing*** in your English exam, there are two main things you need to keep in mind as you plan your writing.

1. Who is the **Audience** that you're writing for?

2. What is the **Purpose** that your writing is trying to fulfil?

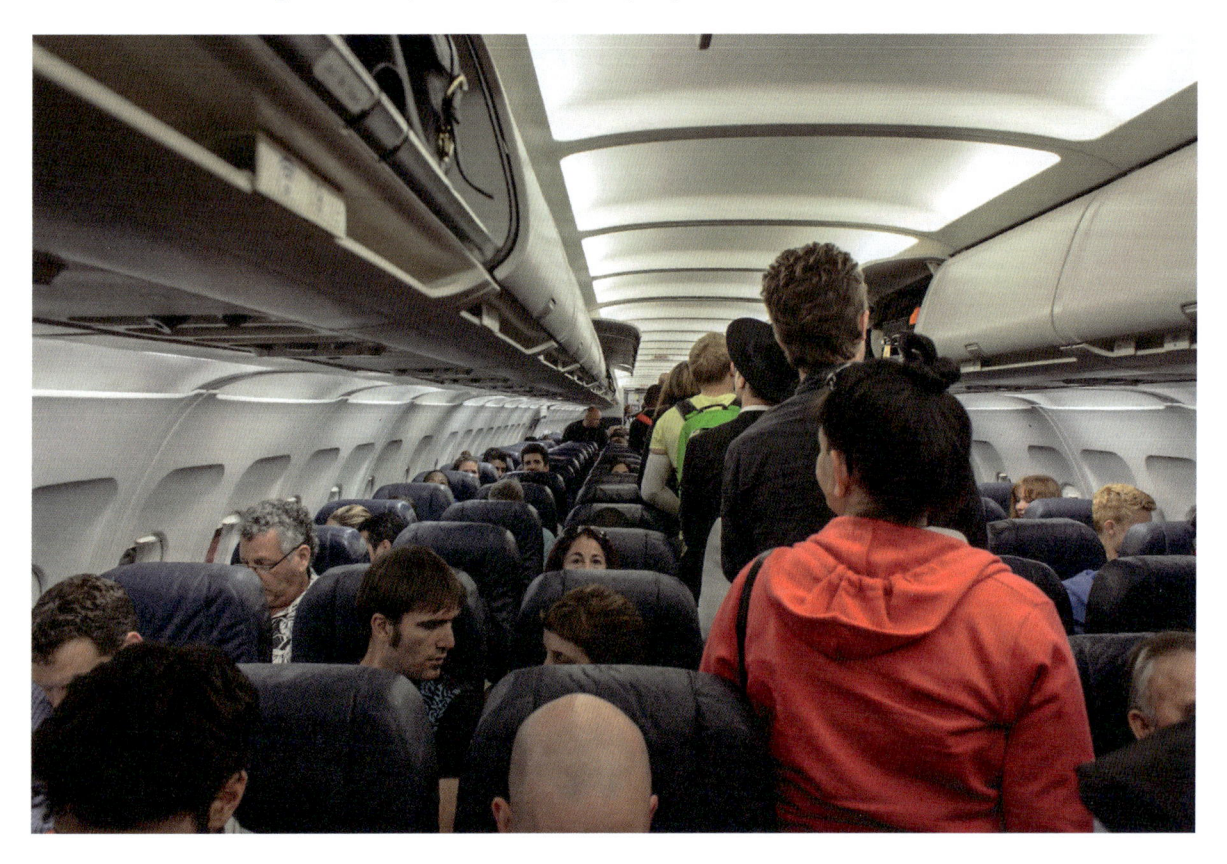

In terms of **Audience** and **Purpose**, this explanation below might help:

Take a look at the photo of the aircraft cabin above, filling up with boarding passengers. It's pretty crowded, but soon everyone will be in their seats, buckling up ready for take-off. Then, as the plane taxis out to the runway, the passengers will be asked to study the aircraft safety card. It's a vital part of any airline's safety procedures and is designed to protect us all as passengers in the case of an emergency.

A typical aircraft safety card may well look like the one shown below.

This is actually quite a good place to start when thinking about **Audience** and **Purpose**.

First, ask yourself who the audience for the aircraft safety card is?

The answer might seem obvious at first – it's the passengers, surely?

Well, yes, *it is* the passengers. But look again at the photo of the aircraft cabin above and ask yourself whether all the passengers are the same?

Of course they're not.

There are male and female passengers for a start. Some are quite young, some a little older. Some are wearing glasses, some not.

And there are one or two things we can't see from the photograph.

For instance, we don't know what nationality the passengers are, or how many might be able to speak English. And we don't even know whether there might be some passengers who are unable to read and write.

As for the *purpose* of the safety card, this was to provide *all* passengers with essential safety advice and guidance. In addition, it's been written and designed to be read speedily. Airline passengers are unlikely to want to spend too long reading about safety so it's important to use that limited time as efficiently and effectively as possible.

Equipped with this simple information about our **Audience** and **Purpose**, take a look at the short exercise below. Look at the image of the safety card above and have a go at jotting down some of its main features.

1 ....

2 ....

3 ....

4 ....

5 ....

Now check your responses with some of mine below:

- The images outnumber the written text significantly
- The information is conveyed sequentially in a cartoon-like format
- Some key information has been translated into several languages
- The colour red has been used to highlight key safety information
- The safety card is quite short

When we think about these features, we can see that the safety card has been written with a diverse *audience* in mind in terms of age, gender, nationality and literacy skills.

Now let's look at another example where a text has been written carefully with **Audience** and **Purpose** clearly and mind.

On 22nd May, 2017, a devastating terrorist attack was carried out at the Manchester Arena. In the aftermath, it was vital that the nation's leaders provide as much **clarity** and **reassurance** as possible for the **people of Manchester** as well as the **population of the country as a whole**.

Here is a transcript of the speech given by the Prime Minister at the time of the attack – Theresa May.

> It is now beyond doubt that the people of Manchester and of this country have fallen victim to a callous terrorist attack.
>
> An attack that targeted some of the youngest people in our society with cold calculation.

This was among the worst terrorist incidents we have ever experienced in the United Kingdom.

And although it is not the first time Manchester has suffered in this way, it is the worst attack the city has experienced and the worst ever to hit the north of England.

The police and security services are working at speed to establish the complete picture. But I want to tell you what I can at this stage.

At 10.33pm last night, police were called to reports of an explosion at Manchester Arena in Manchester city centre, near Victoria train station.

We now know that a single terrorist detonated his improvised explosive device near one of the exits of the venue, deliberately choosing the time and place to cause maximum carnage and kill and injure indiscriminately.

The explosion coincided with the conclusion of a pop concert, which was attended by many young families and groups of children.

All acts of terrorism are cowardly attacks on innocent people but this attack stands out for its appalling, sickening cowardice.

Deliberately targeting innocent defenceless children and young people who should have been enjoying one of the most memorable nights of their lives.

In terms of **Audience**, the speech succeeds for the following reasons:

- It links together the people of Manchester and the population of the U.K. as a whole in the opening sentence; this is a very strong, direct signal in terms of who the Prime Minister was addressing – her *audience*
- The use of the word '*we*' in the 5th line helps to cement a bond with the audience and the reference to "*the United Kingdom*" reinforces the idea that this is for a UK-wide audience and not just for the people of Manchester
- Nevertheless, the reference in the 4th paragraph to "*Manchester*" and the "*north of England*" establish a direct link with the local population too

As for **Purpose**, the Prime Minister's speech covers the following bases:

- A calm, business-like tone throughout suggests the idea of *business as usual* – vital so that terrorism is denied any sense of victory or success
- Sufficient factual information in order to suggest the credibility of the nation's leaders at this time of crisis
- Clear explanations about the work of the police and security services helps to offer the necessary re-assurance to her audience
- Further re-assurance is delivered as a result of the detailed summary and explanation of what had happened
- Finally, the speech ends with an appeal to the audience for strength and resolve in the face of such terrorist attacks

The examples of the aircraft safety card and the transcript of this speech should have given you some insights into how writing with an **audience** and **purpose** in mind can work.

Your GCSE English Language examination will ask you to produce a piece of non-fiction writing with a particular *purpose*. It will probably be one of the following:

- Writing to explain
- Writing to advise or instruct
- Writing to argue
- Writing to persuade

The *audience* is a little less prescribed, however, regardless of the purpose of the non-fiction writing you've been asked to produce, it's likely to be quite formal. This might include:

- A newspaper (typically a broadsheet one) – so a wide, general audience
- An employer/owner of a company
- The head of an organisation – perhaps a charity, a TV channel, or even a headteacher
- A group of students of your own age, in a formal setting, such as a school assembly

The actual question that you'll be given will consist of some combination of *audience* and *purpose*, as well as the specific form or genre you will need to write in. Examples might include the following:

- Write an *article* for a *newspaper* in which you *explain* your views on compulsory national service for all 16 year olds.

Try to write the opening paragraph or two in the space provided below.

....
....
....
....

- Write a ***letter*** to the ***managing director*** of a local company in which you try to ***persuade*** him/her to donate to a charity seeking to improve leisure facilities for teenagers in your community.

Try to write the opening paragraph or two in the space provided below.

- Write a *speech* that you will deliver to your *fellow students* in which you *argue* for one day per week without using social media.

Try to write the opening paragraph or two in the space provided below.

- Write a **leaflet** to be distributed to the **elderly residents** in your community in which you **advise** them how to stay fit and active.

Try to write the opening paragraph or two in the space provided below.

....

....

....

....

....

....

....

....

Finally, remember that *audience* awareness is often overlooked by students in their exams and yet it's a really important part of non-fiction writing.

You should make a point of showing that you are aware of your *audience* throughout your piece of writing by trying to refer to them quite directly as appropriate.

In addition, your argument needs to keep your *audience* in mind at all times and should be targeted at their likely attitudes and concerns.

Section 4

Tone

Tone

Tone is important in any sort of writing, but is actually essential when it comes to non-fiction/transactional writing because we are likely to need to demonstrate our attitude towards a topic, whichever end of the spectrum that might be, from neutral through to being angry or enthusiastic.

As writers, when we pay attention to tone, we are helping to shape and determine what it is our readers detect about what we want to say.

How come?

Because as writers, and readers, we tend to share an agreed understanding of what the words that have been used actually mean, not just on a simple level, but also in terms of any meaning that might lie behind them too.

So here are a few simple rules for using **tone** effectively in your writing:

- It's mainly about your choice of words … think carefully. If in any doubt, try to come up with a range of alternatives and choose the most appropriate to match what it is you want to say and the way you want to say it

- Review each and every sentence that you write and look for any 'weak links' – remember, just one sentence where the words and message jar or don't seem to fit, can ruin the overall impact of the entire piece of writing so do your best to be consistent and thorough all the way through

- Not as easy as it sounds, but try to be true to yourself and write from the heart in terms of how you're trying to answer the particular question; sincerity and honesty will add to your credibility as a writer and to the power of the message you're trying to convey

Below are some examples of my own attempts to write in a range of genres and using a different tone in each case. Take a look and see what you think.

1. Angry

From a ***Letter*** to the local paper about the need for a safe pedestrian crossing at a busy junction.

For far too long, our local politicians have spewed out nothing but lazy excuses for their failure to act and install a pedestrian crossing at the junction of Tilbury Avenue and Greenside Lane. They've wittered about the need to do yet another survey into traffic volume. Nonsense! Three surveys have been carried out already. Let me remind your readers that there have been a dozen horrific accidents at this busy junction in the same period. The politicians simper about the need to consult with local residents. More absurd nonsense! Local residents have been the driving force behind the campaign for a safe crossing and have made their feelings known to the press and the council over and over again. No more excuses. Lives are at risk for goodness sake!

2. Enthusiastic

From a *Speech* to a meeting of a new charity to support talented young artists.

I can't tell you how thrilled I am to have the chance to share with you the latest news about *Art Camp*. As you all know, I've been absolutely passionate, like yourselves, about the idea of giving young people the chance to experience art in exciting and stimulating environments; young people with an abundance of amazing talent who might otherwise be deprived of the chance to grow and develop as artists. So I'm proud, delighted and privileged to tell you that we've now received a huge donation that's going to allow us to plan for the very first *Art Camp* this summer. Well done, everyone – we've done it!

3. Frank/Honest

From a *Leaflet* advising travellers about likely delays at airport check-in due to enhanced security arrangements.

We all know that air travel can be very stressful these days. Nobody wants to be delayed whether you're on business or flying off on holiday. Some delays are inevitable, of course, whether they're due to flight cancellations, poor weather conditions, or crowded airspace.

Sadly, another reality of life for the flying public these days is the need for airport and airline security staff to be even more vigilant than usual in the face of occasional increases in the threat level being posed. And that's what we're faced with at present. Below is a short explanation about what you're likely to experience when you arrive and pass through your local airport and why these more stringent security measures are deemed to be important and effective.

4. Impassioned

From an *Article* outlining your views on the importance of knowing how to complain.

You just know when something's not up to scratch. I'm right, aren't I? And we can all recognise lousy service when we're on the receiving end, yes? I've certainly bought products that are substandard and not *'fit for purpose'* – you too, I'll bet! As for unpalatable food – don't get me going. The list of problems we as consumers face is seemingly endless. So what can we do about it?

Complain, that's what! Complain, then complain some more, and keep up the complaining until you get what you, the paying customer, deserve. Never forget, you have a right to complain. Don't let anyone tell you otherwise.

5. Optimistic

From an *Essay* outlining why you agree with the following statement;
'Gardening is likely to become more popular than ever before in the future.'

Blue skies and sunshine always bring people outdoors and into their gardens. Who wouldn't want to sit on a sun lounger on a carefully cut lawn, surrounded by row upon row of bright, coloured flowers and an abundance of lush plants on a summer's day? People aren't merely soaking up the sun's rays, though. In towns, cities and villages across the country, each generation is discovering the joys of gardening.

Inspired by a range of superb television programmes and with a growing array of plants to choose from in local garden centres, young and old are keen to make the most of their gardens. It doesn't matter whether that's a balcony on a city centre apartment, a small back yard in a terraced house, or a sprawling suburban patch, the thrill and satisfaction that gardening brings is spreading far and wide.

> **Why not have a go at writing a paragraph or two for each of the 5 examples below following the guidelines below:**

No.	Tone	Genre	Title
1	Appreciative	Letter	To Managing Director of local company, thanking him/her for donation to charity supporting project to improve local open play spaces for children.
2	Compassionate	Article	In which you outline your views on the importance of helping to alleviate loneliness among the elderly.
3	Despairing	Essay	In which you disagree with a proposal to remove health warnings from cigarette packets.
4	Forceful	Speech	To school assembly of fellow students, urging them to help provide advice and guidance for younger students to avoid online bullying.
5	Upbeat	Leaflet	To parents, providing advice and ideas for helping their children enjoy the school prom.

1. Appreciative

> From a ***Letter*** to the Managing Director of a local company, thanking him/her for donation to charity supporting project to improve local open play spaces for children.

2. Compassionate

From an *Article* outlining your views on the importance of helping to alleviate loneliness among the elderly.

3. Despairing

From an *Essay* outlining why you disagree with a proposal to remove health warnings from cigarette packets.

4. Forceful

From a *Speech* to a school assembly of fellow students, urging them to help provide advice and guidance for younger students to avoid online bullying.

5. Upbeat

From a *Leaflet* For parents, providing advice and ideas for helping their children enjoy the school prom.

Section 5

Discourse Markers

Discourse Markers

Imagine having to lug a load of paper, cardboard and other materials around like this everyday on the back of your bicycle.

I remember being in awe of this man as he waited to pedal his vehicle across a busy road junction in Hangzhou in China. How was it possible, I thought, for one man to pedal such a bulky and unwieldy load safely? The answer, of course, lay in the fact that he'd paid careful attention to the way he stowed the various parts of his cargo onto the cart attached to his bicycle. Everything needed to be placed in just such a way so that it was all balanced and remained in place.

Now imagine owning and running this roadside bookstore and newsagents in Mumbai in India, and trying to keep track of all the publications you've got available for sale. That's no mean feat.

The owner certainly looks calm enough and could no doubt find exactly what the customer is asking for. Once again, the secret would seem to lie in a carefully organised system, with everything in its place. Otherwise, chaos would ensue.

Both of these images offer helpful visual analogies for thinking about, and understanding, **discourse markers** and how to use them when producing non fiction/transactional writing, whether a letter or a leaflet, an essay, article or speech. The common denominator in each case is the requirement to convey and communicate your ideas, views and opinions clearly and precisely. It's important to remember, too, that your ideas, views and opinions will almost certainly expand and develop in the course of your piece of writing. **Discourse markers** are there to help us to organise, sequence and share our thinking as it reaches the page; thinking which can often be complex and varied as it wends its way through a piece of non fiction writing. The reader is likely to need a little signposting along the way and these can take a variety of forms.

Signposts are on our roads to provide important information such as telling us what the speed limit is in a particular area. They can also warn of potential hazards ahead. The image above illustrates this nicely.

Discourse markers help serve a range of purposes when it comes to aiding the reader in understanding and following a writer's train of thought. These include the following … and in each case, I've provided some examples.

Sorting your ideas and thinking into sections

First, firstly, first of all,

At the outset, in the first place, afterwards,

Providing extra or additional ideas as your thinking develops

Furthermore, in addition, additionally, over and above, on top of this,

Moreover, besides,

Reflect on your ideas and contrast with what you have previously written

On the one hand, on the other hand,

Nevertheless, nonetheless,

However, in fact, yet, actually, although

Pulling your ideas and thinking together and generalising

To some extent,

Generally, in general, generally speaking,

On the whole, in most cases

Showing examples and exceptions in your thinking and ideas

For example, for instance,

In particular, et cetera (etc)

Showing likely consequences and outcomes

As a result, in which case, in that case,

Consequently, therefore, so, then,

Gathering together and re-stating your ideas and views

In other words, in short,

Some examples of discourse markers in action:

1. *Second*, their increasingly desperate efforts to preserve their grip on power are having increasingly extreme consequences.
2. *Nonetheless*, it is possible to see what the headline writer was clumsily reaching for, which is the shocking incongruity of it all.
3. *In short*, you have to be prepared to be thought a fool.
4. *Unsurprisingly*, considering stages can last up to six hours, there is often very little going on as the peloton meanders through the picturesque countryside from one town to the next, a whirring, shape-shifting swarm of arrestingly garish lycra-clad human endeavour.
5. *So* it's rubbish, but well presented rubbish nevertheless.

Now you try to use some of the following discourse markers at the start of a sentence. Write in the boxes below.

First..
....
....

On the one hand..
....
....

In most cases...
....
....

As a result

In other words

SECTION 6
PLANNING

Planning

Did I mention that I make the *best* spaghetti bolognese? It's my speciality and I've cooked it so many times I reckon I could make it with my eyes shut.

If I'm honest, though, I do follow a clear method, and the most important part of this for me is getting all the ingredients prepared in advance; peel and chop an onion; chop some garlic finely; season the meat; boil some water ready for the spaghetti; prepare some fresh herbs; and so it goes.

The preparation and the cooking sequence that follows are the key to the success of the dish. What's this got to do with the **non-fiction writing** task on your GCSE English Language examination? It's a bit like cooking. If you check you have all the ingredients before you start making the dish, you won't suddenly find halfway through that you're missing a vital ingredient.

You'll know right from the start whether or not you have everything you need or whether you'll need to go out and get something. You need to do the same thing before you start writing!

Don't skimp on the planning stage

Exams can be quite stressful, not least because you're working against the clock. You need to manage your time carefully to maximise your scores. Under these circumstances, it can be really tempting to skimp on the planning and preparation stage of your writing. My advice would certainly be to budget for time at the start of the **non-fiction writing** question to carry out some planning. It can make all the difference to the content, structure and overall quality of your piece of writing.

Producing a piece of non-fiction writing – an *article, essay, leaflet, letter* or *speech* – is not like running the 100 metres sprint where speed is of the essence. You need to be more considered and reflective.

It's one thing to acknowledge the need to plan but the tricky bit is actually doing the planning and understanding *how* to plan!

How to Plan – Part One

- Allow up to **5 minutes** or so for thinking and planning; it's time well spent!
- Think carefully about the question and the specifics of the **non fiction writing** task you've been asked to tackle
- In particular, think about what form of writing it is, and what the audience and purpose are for the writing
- Now think about the overall outline for your writing – in particular, think about your introduction and conclusion
- Try to decide whether you agree or disagree with the topic in the question; what does your instinct tell you?
- Jot down as many ideas as you can in relation to the topic you've been asked to write about – don't try to force this part of the process – try to allow your ideas to flow naturally

How to Plan – Part Two

- By now you should have produced a list of ideas relating to the topic you've been asked to write about
- Try to make some sense of all the ideas you've pulled together; try to arrange them in some sort of logical sequence – whatever works best for you – this might be chronological, sequential or grouped according to different sorts of ideas and material
- Now take a fresh look back over your ideas list and make any adjustments that you think might be helpful – it's surprising what you might notice on a second, closer look!
- Remember that planning is all about organising your ideas in a coherent, logical and sensible structure so they can be communicated as clearly as possible to the reader – so have another quick look over your ideas and the order you've arranged them into and think about how well they'll meet your audience's needs

Whatever Works Best For You

The way you jot down and arrange your ideas is entirely up to you. It's really important that you do whatever works best for you.

For some students a **spider diagram** of their ideas might be appropriate.

Spider diagrams are particularly useful for students who find that a visual approach works for them.

Spider diagrams can also be really useful for helping to arrange the various aspects of your thinking into different categories or sections.

Here's one I produced to help me to write down my views about some pedestrianisation proposals for a town centre. I've used abbreviations and listed my ideas using just a few key words.

See what you think:

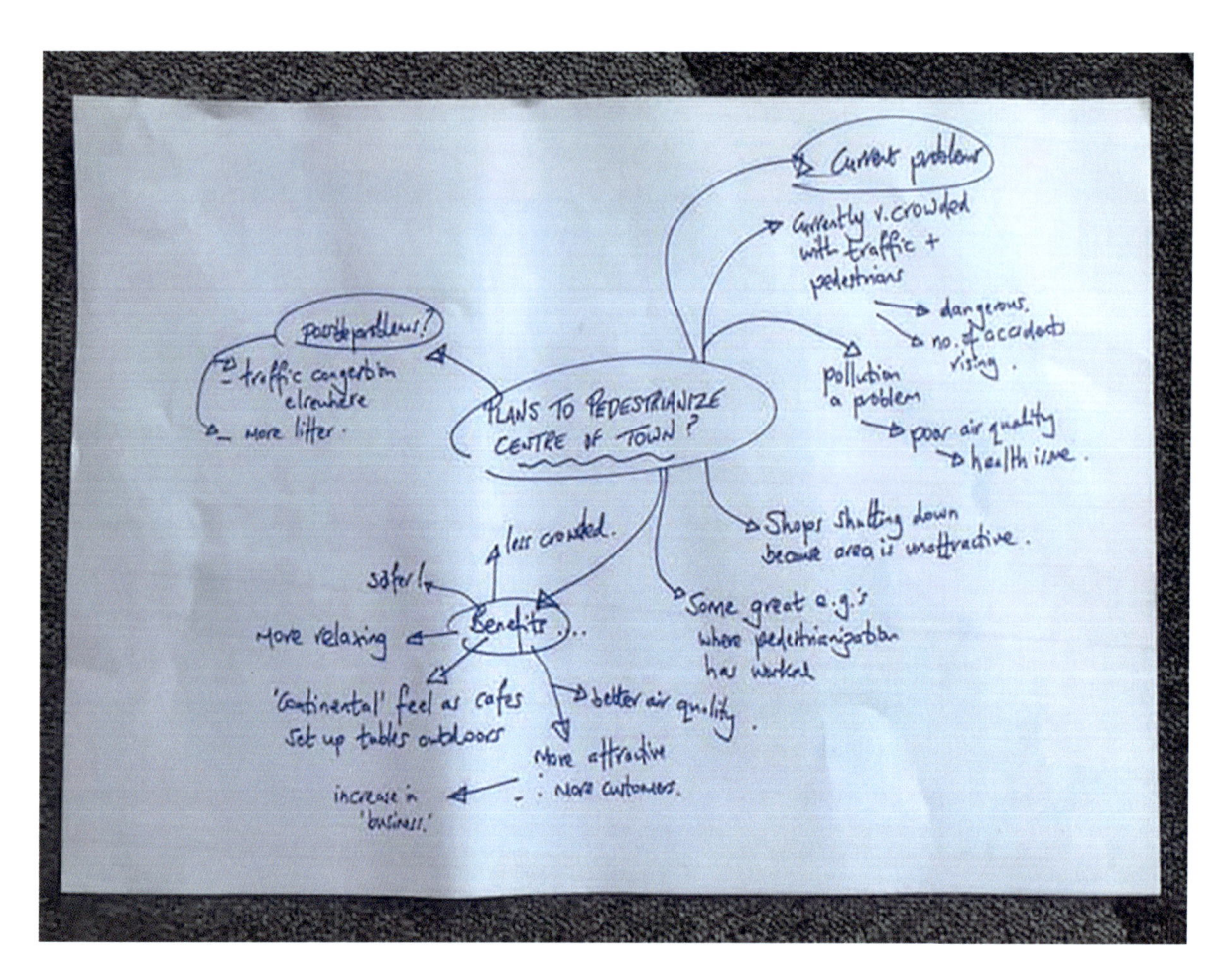

I've placed the topic that I need to address in my piece of **non-fiction writing** right at the centre of the diagram. In addition, I've created two key headings – *current problems* and *benefits* – as well as anticipating the sort of arguments someone with the opposite viewpoint might have under the heading *possible problems*.

You can also see from my spider diagram that I'm in favour of the pedestrianisation proposals and have plenty of ideas to support this viewpoint. In fact, my ideas in support of the proposal probably make up around 85- 90% of what I've included on the spider diagram.

Now Have A Go Yourself

Here's a non-fiction writing question for you to have a think about:

> *'Who needs Libraries any more when we can get all the information we need off the internet?'*
>
> **Write an article for a broadsheet newspaper in which you explain your point of view on this statement.**

First – think about the question and jot down whatever ideas come into your mind in a simple list below.

....

....

....

....

....

....

....

....

....

Second – take a minute or two to look back over the ideas you've jotted down in the list above.

Now decide which side of the argument you're on and organise your ideas into a spider diagram using the space below. I've included a few shapes that I thought might be useful for you. Feel free to adapt as you see fit. Don't forget to use arrows or lines to help connect your ideas on the diagram.

Time devoted to planning will certainly help with the sequencing of your ideas. Ideally, this sequence should also help to build a sense of momentum for the reader/examiner.

Ideally, the way you sequence your ideas in a piece of **non fiction writing** should draw the reader/examiner into an argument that is increasingly convincing and compelling; a more positive sense of a complete argument should gradually emerge in your writing. This should ultimately lead to a carefully structured conclusion to round off your argument.

Plan And Write With An Audience In Mind

Naturally, your planning should always take into account who your audience is as this will help to determine the way you set out your ideas and opinions. Once you know who the audience for your piece of non-fiction writing is, you can start to consider what sort of thoughts they might have already with regard to the topic you're going to be writing about.

This might also help you to think through the sort of ideas and arguments they might want to make; with this in mind, you can anticipate their potential response/s and set out your counter-arguments more clearly and effectively.

You don't need to make things too complicated when you do this. You could, for example, write something like;

> *"I'm sure you probably believe that public libraries are an expensive luxury that we can't afford, however …"*

Or;

> *"Even though there are likely to be many people like yourself who take the view that libraries are an expensive luxury that we can't afford, there is plenty of evidence to suggest that …"*

Planning To Be Accurate

Although the main focus of your planning is going to be on generating and organising your content into an effective argument or viewpoint, you should also keep in mind that there are quite a few marks available for accuracy too.

In particular, you should think about planning to use a range, or variety, of punctuation, in your piece of non-fiction/transactional writing.

The simplest thing might just be to write out each of the pieces of punctuation that are at your disposal and keep this as an *aide-memoire* or crib sheet for you to quickly refer back to as you complete your piece of writing.

Capital Letter	A	Lower Case Letter	a
Full Stop	.	Comma	,
Question Mark	?	Exclamation Mark	!
Semi-Colon	;	Colon	:
Inverted Commas	" "	Ellipsis	…
Dash	—		

Apostrophe (possession/missing letter):

The girl's shoes   *can't*

Non Fiction Writing Exemplars

Write an Article

> *"Social media has a completely negative effect on people's lives and should be banned."*
>
> **Write an article for a broadsheet newspaper in which you explain your point of view with regard to this statement.**

It's all about improving people's #social lives

I've lost count of the number of times I get asked whether I've got a banking app on my phone when I go into the local branch of my bank. These days, there's an assumption that we're all happy to carry out basic functions such as banking on our phones. Yet for some reason, it's not alright to use social media apps on our phones. Some people, who might happily accept that we use banking apps appear to feel that using social media is going to have a negative effect on our lives and should be banned. I beg to differ.

The Danger of Dwindling Direct Contact

It's not just online banking, of course. How many of us have ordered books, clothes, or trainers online? A hasty signature at the door on the delivery driver's phone is about all the social contact an online retail purchase entails. With so much of our lives now online, we're in real danger of losing those all-important social interactions as direct contact with our fellow human beings starts to dwindle.

Incidental, daily contact with people is vital to us all as human beings, whether it's a quick chat with a fellow dog-walker in the park, a moan about the weather to the person next to us on the bus, or a smile and a **thank you** *to the barista serving us with a cup of coffee. Our daily lives are all the richer for being alongside other people every now and again.*

Friendships Are Precious

*As for our friendships, these are precious and have a massive impact on our wellbeing. They can take our feelings of happiness to another level altogether. So with friendship at such a premium, why would anyone want to deny people all over the world the chance to maintain and nurture their friendships through social media? What could be better than sharing news of your recent life experiences on something like **Facebook** – not to mention some photographs too – with all of your friends at the click of a button?*

Likes, Shares and Follows

*It's easy for some people to dismiss the social media phenomenon of **likes, shares,** and **follows**, as trivial, meaningless and encouraging addictive behaviours, but to do so overlooks the affirmation such online gestures bring. It helps us to recognise that there are people out there who share our views, understand our feelings, and value us as individuals. Banning social media would remove this positive and important dimension that it brings to our lives.*

Stay Connected

*For some, active use of the online news and social networking service, **Twitter**, enables them to feel more connected to news events, locally, nationally and internationally. While there is undoubtedly concern about some of the verbal abuse that can take place on **Twitter**, this is easily outweighed by giving people of all ages and backgrounds, the opportunity for direct interaction with people they'd never have dreamt of being able to connect with. As for abuse, **Twitter** users always have the option of **blocking, muting** or **unfollowing** other users.*

Bringing Economic Benefits

*Leaving aside **Facebook** and **Twitter**, new social media platforms are making their mark all the time, not least with the younger generation. Two really good examples of this would be **Instagram** and **TikTok**, both of which are essentially all about visual content – videos and images – which can be posted and shared easily. In the case of **Instagram**, in particular, there has been a strong trend towards online advertising and marketing for young people, often deploying 'influencers' – social media users who have the power to affect the purchase decisions of others because of their authority, knowledge, position or relationship with their audience. Banning the likes of **Instagram** could even have a negative effect on the global economy these days!*

The World Has Changed

*Banning social media is simply not an option anymore; the world has changed and with it, the way we do things. Nowhere is this more apparent than in the case of **YouTube**. While some people might not necessarily see **YouTube** as a social media platform, it clearly is as it fulfils a number of the key criteria for being one. This includes enabling users to upload content freely onto personalised sites. It also enables conversations and comments between those viewing the videos and the person who made and uploaded them.*

*This only tells part of the story of the value of **YouTube** as a social media platform though. In the case of social media in general, according to a recent survey, 94 percent of teenagers who go online using a mobile device do so daily. **YouTube**, **Instagram** and **TikTok** are the most popular online platforms among teens. 95% of teenagers now have access to a smartphone, and 45% say they are online 'almost constantly'.*

In Conclusion

*The evidence is convincing about the many benefits that social media affords. We're living in an increasingly connected world as a result of the technologies that facilitate social media; who would want to deny current and future generations the opportunity to lead fuller, richer, more engaged social lives as a result? To focus on the **'negative effects'** of social media is to join the ranks of the people over the course of history who have condemned mankind's attempts to fly or to send missions to Mars; or the people who balked at the advance of the machines in the cotton mills during the Industrial Revolution. The world is moving on and any attempt to ban social media is doomed to fail as surely as any attempt to swim against the tide.*

Commentary

- There is a clear, bold headline that sums up the overall viewpoint contained within the article as a whole
- The opening paragraph provides some context as well as concluding with a clear statement of which side of the argument the article is on
- There are regular sub-headings used throughout to help signpost the direction of the argument and viewpoint in the article
- The article is carefully structured as it moves from a general exploration of the importance of friendship and social contact to more specific paragraphs that deal with some of the most popular current social media platforms and the benefits they bring

- Rhetorical questions have been used in a thought-provoking manner in both the fourth and in the final paragraph
- The article acknowledges potential arguments that align with the statement in the question at the start
- The article then goes on to address these potential arguments with counter-arguments, for example, in the fifth paragraph, where the article makes a strong point about the value of *Likes, Shares* and *Follows*
- A further example where the article acknowledges, then counters an opposing viewpoint is in the 6th paragraph; here the argument about the possibility of online abuse on *Twitter* is countered with the argument that *Twitter* users have the option of muting or blocking anyone perceived to be abusive
- A strong concluding paragraph makes some powerful summative comments in rounding off the article's viewpoint, leaving the reader in no doubt as to where the article's sympathies lie

Instagram : @secretsofenglish

Write an Essay

"Teenagers need to become more active if they are to lead healthier lives."

Write an essay, explaining why you agree or disagree with the statement.

Who couldn't get used to sitting down all day? Whether in school in front of the teacher, at home in front of the tv, or on the bus surrounded by friends and phones; it's all too easy to lead a sedentary life these days. The net result, though, is that the average teenager just isn't getting anywhere near enough exercise. They're sacrificing their future health and well-being for the comforts of the couch.

So what's the problem?

First, it's very shortsighted. Of course, when we're young, older age seems an eternity away; it's not something that's going to happen to us, is it? The evidence, however, is clear in showing that a lack of physical activity can impede the healthy growth and development of teenagers and have a significant negative effect on overall well-being. Worse still, it can be responsible for causing many long-term health problems – both physical and mental – as we become adults.

It gets worse. In some cases, a chronic lack of exercise and physical activity as a teenager can even lead to reduced life expectancy. Yes, that's right, it can lead to reduced life expectancy! Scary, eh? Yet almost certainly this is not even remotely on the radar for the average 15 or 16 year old. After all, what harm can another hour's binge-viewing do us when all's said and done?

The problem is often exacerbated, though, by a surge in obesity, as well as the current trend towards unhealthy eating. With the ready availability of calorie-laden snacks and fizzy drinks, life on the sofa just gets more and more attractive. Yet the hard truth is that as teenagers we need to take at least 60 minutes of physical activity every day. Is it just me, or are you hearing the theme music to **'Mission Impossible'** *at this stage too?*

The statistics point to the scale of the challenge with just 15% of girls aged 11 to 15 in England managing to take 60 minutes of daily exercise. Although the boys do a little better on 22%, there's no room for complacency here either. On top of this, only one in three children of this age are taking part in any organised sport outside school, according to the figures, presented to the International Congress on Physical Activity and Public Health.

Perhaps it's not all gloom and doom though. Statistics for future sales of wearable fitness device, FitBit, show a massive increase; by 2022, it is predicted that this market is going to grow to nearly 200 million units. These customers are likely to be the teenagers of today, so maybe they're more aware of their health than we give them credit for.

As someone who walks to school every day, it's also clear to me that this is a great form of moderate exercise that a majority of teenagers take every day without even realising it. It's the same walking the family dog too; teenagers can often be spotted out with their hound in the neighbourhood or local park.

While I'm not underestimating the value and importance of any of these forms of exercise, I still think it's a matter of great concern that active lifestyles are really not being led. All too often, any physical activity happens on a haphazard basis which does little to have a positive impact on the overall health and well-being of teenagers.

In conclusion, the current score line in the contest between exercise and inactivity would seem to be 5-nil to the couch. Certainly, the statistics about teenage exercise levels and healthy lifestyles display a worrying negative trend. It seems clear that my fellow teenagers need a hefty push to get them off their couches and onto the pavements, paths and parks if they're to lead the sort of healthy lives that are going to protect their well-being in the long term.

Commentary

- Effective introduction – starts with a rhetorical question – which challenges the reader from the very first line of the essay
- Followed by several bold statements which set out my stall clearly – that I don't believe teenagers are getting anything like the right amount of exercise for a healthy life
- Rule of three – used in the second sentence of the essay – to convey the widespread nature of the problem of teenage inactivity
- More rhetorical question/s – "So what's the problem?"
- An 'explain' question so the tone of the writing has become a little gentler as I'm not trying to persuade my reader to change his/her mind

- Use of facts and figures in the mid-section of the essay help to build the credibility of my case
- Well organised ideas in the mid-section of the essay which expand on, and illustrate, the argument/s I've set out in my introduction; the mid-section shows a logical sequence of thought
- The organisation of my ideas into a clear sequence is assisted by the use of linking words and phrases, eg; *however, first…, worse still, It gets worse, Yet almost certainly, Perhaps, …*
- Effective, well written paragraphs – each one beginning with a clear topic sentence and containing one main idea
- Short sentences for dramatic emphasis – to stress serious the nature of things
- Humour – reference to 'Mission Impossible' theme
- Recognises and dismisses opposing arguments – but otherwise it's just a presentation of ideas
- Ending – that summarises my thoughts + refers to the key words in the title – and shows the reader that I've delivered on what I set out to do at the start
- Wording in the final paragraph signposts I'm pulling my thoughts together –

  "In conclusion …"

Write a Leaflet

Write a leaflet for visitors that explains how to get the best out of their visit to a local attraction.

Not Just Another Visit To 'Another Place'

What's all the fuss about?

It's been nearly 15 years since the spectacular art installation – 'Another Place' – arrived on Crosby Beach, about 7 miles north of the city of Liverpool. Since then, the installation which consists of 100 cast iron, life-size statues standing at apparently random spots on the beach – has attracted thousands of visitors from far and wide. Standing eerily looking out to sea – sometimes even standing in the sea when the tide is in – these figures almost look like something out of 'Dr Who'; perhaps it's this eerie quality that draws people.

Most visitors seem strangely drawn to these silent witnesses to the sea's different moods. Some people stand and stare back at them, while others relish the chance for a creative selfie or two. It's not uncommon to find that previous visitors have decorated one or more of the figures with hats, scarves and other items which adds to the surreal nature of the place.

How to get there

Lots of visitors to Liverpool make sure they include a trip to Crosby Beach as part of their itinerary – after all, it's only a short drive away. You can also get a local train from Liverpool to Blundellsands and Crosby Station – after that, it's only a 10 minute walk away. Here's the address; Mariners Road, Crosby Beach, Liverpool, Merseyside, L23 6SX

When to visit

It's really up to you when you visit as this is a public beach. Although a warm, sunny day can be great, sometimes a winter's day when the skies are dark and threatening can be really atmospheric and a perfect, moody backdrop for the figures dotted around the beach.

You need to remember that this is a beach on the open sea and that it's subject to tides that can affect the amount of beach you can access. We'd recommend that you consult a reliable website such as TidesChart – https://bit.ly/2J61nfH

Don't be put off by a high tide though – it can be fascinating to see a number of the figures partly submerged – sometimes it's only the head and shoulders that remain above the water!

A Word Of Warning

Crosby Beach is a non-bathing beach with areas of soft sand and mud and a risk of changing tides. You should aim to stay within 50 metres of the promenade whatever the tide and not attempt to walk out to the furthest figures. Lifeguards are on duty in the area.

On A Brighter Note

Naturally the main attraction for visitors to 'Another Place' are the enigmatic figures dotted around the beach; it's like nothing you've ever seen before.

It's also great for the following:

- *Taking a walk in the fresh air and blowing the cobwebs away – perhaps with the family dog in tow!*
- *Photography – not just the iron figures – there's also the wide open stretches of the beach itself as well as the views out to sea, including the Wirral Peninsula and the Welsh coast*
- *Watch the ships sailing in and out of the River Mersey – you'll be surprised how many there are*
- *Now and again, there'll be charity walks along this stretch of the beach – it's great to join in if you get the chance*
- *Whatever the weather, there's nothing better than having an ice-cream by the seaside*

Don't just take it from me – here's what some visitors have said

'Having been told about this place by a friend, we decided to head out to Liverpool and see these statues and add them to our memories. We were totally surprised and blown away by the scenery – it was like being abroad! I was amazed by the golden sands. An enjoyable day out for the family.'

'Back again. We just love it here. Lots of wide open space. Love the iron men. Fresh air, good walk, great art, sea and sand, what's not to love.'

'So glad I came here. Really close to Liverpool too. The tide comes in really fast which meant that some of the statues became submerged which was really cool.'

What are you waiting for?

Commentary

- The leaflet has a clear, bold headline at the start – it also uses a slight play on words to engage the reader
- The leaflet has a series of sub-headings all the way through
- Effectively sequenced paragraphs
- Bullet points have been used when appropriate – they take the place of a list
- There is plenty of information for the reader – facts and figures
- The leaflet addresses the reader directly throughout – eg, "It's really up to you when you visit…"
- The leaflet uses a reassuring tone throughout to help guide and explain the local attraction to potential visitors
- A simple range of adjectives designed to appeal to the senses – eg, "warm, sunny day…" and "skies are dark and threatening…"
- Additional useful information including an address and a URL

Please note: I've included a few photographs to show you a little of what Another Place at Crosby Beach looks like. You will not be expected, or able to do so when asked to write a leaflet in the examination.

Write a Letter

Write a letter to the managing director of a local company requesting sponsorship to help purchase 100 new bicycles for use by the public across your town or city.

132, Docklands Road,
Strandside,
Liverpool,
L1 1AB

14th June 2020

Mr Gilbert
Managing Director
The Framework Group Ltd
28 Albert Street
Liverpool
L77 3JK

Dear Mr Gilbert,

I'm writing to seek your company's financial support for an expansion in the number of bicycles available for members of the public across the city. As a major local employer with an excellent track record in assisting health and wellbeing charities and other organisations, locally and nationwide, I felt that the expansion of this important initiative could well be something you might be willing to consider for possible sponsorship.

I realise that you must receive numerous requests similar to this one, but I feel that there are a number of clear reasons why sponsoring the expansion of the number of bicycles across the city would make a significant difference to the daily lives of the people of Liverpool. Ultimately, all of these reasons can be summed up in one short phrase – the health and well-being – of all local citizens from across the entire city. Surely there can be no greater priority for us all.

An expansion of the aforementioned initiative will deliver a clear and immediate result – more people able to ride bicycles – whether as part of a daily commute to college or work, or as a means of making the most of their leisure time. And more people riding bicycles, more regularly, means more people leading healthier lives.

What sort of healthier lives? There are numerous potential benefits. The most obvious one is the improvement in people's cardio-vascular health as cycling raises heart and breathing rates. In a city that's been plagued by heart and lung-related health issues above the national average, cycling can make quite a difference to helping turn the statistics in a more positive direction.

Better still, people who take to cycling reduce their waistlines by burning up more calories on a regular basis; cycling at a speed between 12 and 14 mph helps a 175-pound person burn about 346 calories, according to HealthStatus. The same person burns about 420 calories in 30 minutes of pedalling at a pace of 14 to 16 mph. It's hard to ignore such powerful evidence isn't it?

And on the subject of things we can't ignore when it comes to public health, there's the important matter of reducing the amount of co2 emissions coming from cars on our city's roads. The more people willing and able to cycle, instead of sitting in a car or taxi, the fewer cars there will be on our roads, and the fewer the co2 emissions as a result. Who wouldn't want their children to breathe fresher air into their tender lungs?

The phrase I used earlier in my letter was health and well-being when citing the benefits of more people being able to access bicycles. In terms of well-being, surely being able to cycle around the city at liberty in order to access its many facilities and attractions – its parks, museums, and coastal paths to name just a few – is bound to have a sizeable positive impact on levels of well-being among people as a whole.

Should your company be able to sponsor the expansion of the public bicycles initiative, naturally, you will have all the advertising and marketing benefits this will bring as a result of your name and logo featuring on all the bicycles and at all the parking stations around the city. More gratifying still will surely be the knowledge that your company has been able to make a tangible difference to the lives – the health and well-being – of people from across our amazing city.

I do hope that after careful consideration you might be in a position to help

    Yours sincerely

    M Wheeler

    M. Wheeler

Commentary

- My address written clearly at the top right of the letter
- The date written after a line's gap underneath my address on the right
- The address of the person I'm writing to on the left of the letter, a line or two down from the date, which is on the right
- This is a formal letter – a request for sponsorship funding – so it begins with a formal greeting to the managing director – 'Dear Mr Gilbert'
- Immediately after this, I've 'indented' and started my first paragraph a centimetre or so to the right
- Clear, coherent and sequential paragraphs
- I've also been able to include a few facts and statistics to boost the credibility of the request in my letter
- One or two carefully used rhetorical questions designed to politely challenge the thinking of the person I've written the letter to
- Formal language use in my choice of vocabulary
- Varied sentence structures used appropriately
- I've rounded the letter off with a final appeal for sponsorship funding
- Because I know the name of the person I'm writing to – 'Mr Gilbert' – I've ended my letter with the words 'Yours sincerely'
- Underneath this, I've used my signature, followed by my name and initial printed out – 'M.Wheeler'

Write a Speech

"Green spaces have never been more important in our towns and cities."

Write a speech for an environmental conference in which you explain why you think local parks are more vital than ever.

Good morning, everyone.

I'm Lucy and I'd like to thank you for the invitation to speak at today's event at your conference centre in this amazing setting.

I couldn't help noticing just how many varieties of trees lined the entrance as I walked up the driveway this morning. It's very encouraging to see that some architects are thinking carefully about the natural environment when they're designing modern buildings.

Which brings me to what I want to talk to you about today – the future of our local parks.

I thought a little history might help at the start.

The first publicly-funded park in the world was actually Birkenhead Park on the Wirral, near Liverpool, which was opened as far back as 1847. With the populations of our major cities filling up fast in the Victorian era, living conditions were cramped and crowded and the air in the streets and alleyways was choking.

Fortunately the leaders of our great cities in times gone by had the wisdom and foresight to recognise the dangers to public health and wellbeing and committed to the design and construction of our local parks.

Nearly two centuries later and our parks are in danger as budgets are cut and councils struggle to commit to them as they've always done in the past. Precious green space comes with a price tag it seems. One man's park is another man's prime land for property development.

*What would **you** rather have – trees or tarmac?*

*We all know that cash is in short supply in our local councils. This has created a **cutback culture**, leading to the impression that parks are a luxury that we can no longer afford. So instead of finding creative ways to invest in these vital open spaces, our local politicians have taken the easy way out and chosen to manage the decline of our local parks.*

Although they won't thank me for reminding them, most of the current politicians will be forgotten within the next decade, while many of the trees in our parks have been around for centuries. There's one in my local park that's actually been around for a thousand years – predating the park even!

Timelines tell their own story. Scientific knowledge and evidence about the environment has made slow, careful progress forward. Our temporary politicians are too ready to side-step this in favour of the recent, damaging conclusions of the accountants. With scientists warning us that air pollution is now at record levels, who in their right mind would hand over these established green spaces to the developers' diggers?

The world of science itself uses two key optical devices when carrying out their research – the microscope and the telescope. The microscope can look at the detail *on the ground and the telescope can help us take a much bigger view – it can help us look at entire galaxies if we need to. Imagine harnessing the power of the microscope **and** the telescope together to help find the sort of solutions that will see our local parks thriving in the future.*

It's time for us all to take the blinkers off and look through both lenses and recognise the huge value of our local parks in the lives of local people?

It's up to us to devise a bold, creative and long term manifesto for the preservation and development of our local parks.

A manifesto that uses all the best research and scientific knowledge available in the interests of local people up and down the land.

Most important of all, it'll need to be a manifesto for our generation and for generations to come.

Commit today to making a manifesto for our local parks become a reality!

Commentary

- Introduction – writer introduces herself
- Sets the scene and outlines the issue to be spoken about
- Direct address to audience – regular use of *you* and *your*
- 3 part structure – beginning, mid-section, conclusion
- Anecdotes
- Factual evidence
- Alliteration – eg, cramped, crowded, choking; park, prime, property
- Rhetorical questions – *trees* or *tarmac*?
- Establishes connection with audience/ direct appeal to the audience – through use of personal pronoun – 'we'
- Conclusion and *call to action*

Printed in Great Britain
by Amazon